ARCTIC ELEGIES

Peter Davidson was born in Scotland in 1957 and educated there, and at the Universities of Cambridge and York. He is Senior Research Fellow of Campion Hall, University of Oxford, and Fellow-Curator of the Hall's art collection. As well as many academic works he has published several books of literary non-fiction: *The Idea of North* (2005), *Distance and Memory* (2013), *The Last of the Light* (2015), and *The Lighted Window* (2021). This is his second collection for Carcanet.

Arctic Elegies

PETER DAVIDSON

CARCANET POETRY

First published in Great Britain in 2022 by
Carcanet
Alliance House, 30 Cross Street
Manchester, M2 7AQ
www.carcanet.co.uk

A CIP catalogue record for this book is
available from the British Library.

ISBN 978 1 80017 263 0

Book design by Andrew Latimer
Printed in Great Britain by SRP Ltd, Exeter, Devon

The publisher acknowledges financial
assistance from Arts Council England.

CONTENTS

AD MAIOREM DEI GLORIAM

JACOBITE SONG

The falcon flown, far in the starving air
So many lost, this long, half-secret war.

The regiments like snow all overborne
The boat rowed far from the cold shore, long gone.

O blackbird taken in the fowler's snare
He is now far who will return no more.

The burn is frozen and the bird is flown
The rose is withered and the tower is down.

Snow, falcon, blackbird, water, rose and tower:
Faded, flown, taken, frozen, fallen, gone.

LORD DERWENTWATER'S ROSE

The north is gone now. Victory in loss –
Devotion to the best, most-injured King:
The scaffold stairs shine forth a path of stars,
The blade the rose's thorn in the hand of God.

VENICE GLASSES I

For Victoria Crowe

Thoughts on the City

Seek all you have lost in twilights and depths of mirrors:
Horizons turned dusk and smoke, sanguine and lavender;
Red dust of August blown on the offshore wind,
The first lamps flickering out from the fading quays;
When vanished things take shape in the stir of the waters,
When glimpses and shadows pass at the edges of glasses.

CATTERLINE

For John Morrison

Fifty years past in the wash and the fall of the tides
Below the houses like a crescent moon
Shining above the bay. Harvests and storms;
The smells of limewash, fish-guts, barley straw,
Salt, tar and tidewrack, fifty years ago.

The Sugar-loaf rock was my fortress on the shore
The summer boats pulled up in the long grass,
Yarrow and cresses, fifty years ago;
Bees on the Reath in failing daylight flew
Their silver missions through the golden light,
Nets stretched at night to catch the rising moon.

The barn was black at the foot of our garden
Where Angus painted in the tarry dark
Held prisoner of the tank-trap of the war.
Outside my father worked on in the light,
Painting the yard with night, the house with day;
Or shaped his coloured worlds for me, his son:
Whitening the breakers of dun autumn tides,
Touching red morning to the clouds for me,
Charcoaled those winter afternoons of snow.
I woke to the crack of footfalls on the road,
Hobnails on frosted cobbles, hammering sparks,
Kindling the daybreak from the icy lane.

Storms shadowed hills, the landward clouds took flame
When they took the barley in at the summer's end.
Amongst the stooks they sat on kitchen chairs,
Painting the light and fire: standing there quiet
Beside the last cow-parsley's ragged tower
Watching the bay and the waves and the westering day.
Now they are gone into the evening, where they are gone
They are one with the dusk and the voices of the sea.

We are good children on our journey home,
Home on the cliff path, fifty years ago –
Nothing is lost, I was and I am now–
Dowered as I am with silver of the poor;
My true inheritance my father's distances
Indigo ridges, azure in the far;
The parks of barley falling to the sea
The August kingdoms of the harvest star.

MACNAUGHTAN'S BOOKSHOP, HADDINGTON PLACE, EDINBURGH

Exigent spinster mistress Edinburgh,
Thin wind-bride with your stone-cold mural crown,
What consolations do you show your votaries?
Vast freezing rooms, this fortalice of books?

This shop's the city in epitome:
Its curving windows and its trim-cut stairs;
Inside, dim labyrinths of folios,
A back room full of quarto shelves of Scotland,
The August pleasures of dead advocates:
Bright moors, quick rivers; summer lands north of the Spey.

Let us stroll through the New Town squares at dusk:
Unshuttered windows, distance-coloured walls
Painted rain grey, smoke green, or cloudy rose,
Where lamplight shines on the rows on rows of books.
As frost comes down on streets of libraries:
These wintery precincts of enlightenment
Which hold out for the moment, just, they hold.

BLACK ISLE MADRIGAL

So far, so late, so distant and so cold
How faint the mountains in the fading day.
North of the waters, snow down to the shore,
South of the waters, stone fields, storm blown thorns.
Frost with the dusk now, and night winds that move
Over vast waters from the guardian stars.

SHAKESPEARE'S WINTER'S TALE

This is the fable of the dead
Prince whose parents act his dreams;
It was written by the red
Firelight's dying gleams.

It was evening and colours
Of things he saw were dim;
He wrote of sufferings of mortals
As a child might dream such things.

Winter nights all white and still:
Silver river-mist shakes
And gathers, rising chill,
Purifies, distills at daybreak.

Softly at the curtained windows,
(Candle flame, morning star)
Springs the secret kingdom's dawning
Florizel and Perdita.

After Martinus Nijhoff

VENICE GLASSES II

Vapour trail

After such sorrow, ice and viridian,
The flightless angel on midwinter grass,
Snow overbearing, air gone thin with cold;
Comes this last throw of the departing sun,
Treeline in afterglow, the tawny slopes
Bright with lost days. A vapour trail above –
One scrape of radiance through the dark of things.

ARCTIC ELEGY

For the Franklin Expedition of 1845-48

I.

Ice in the twilight, drift in the bitter night
Thin, broken starlight over the stone shores;
Snow-smoke and ice-mist shimmer in winter air
Over infinities of frozen sea.

Wonderful is the patience of the snow
And glorious the violence of the cold.
How lovely is the power of the dark pole
To draw the iron and move the compass rose.

As cold as loss as cold as freezing steel,
The charts are blank the place is very full;
The ice grows downwards building in the dark,
There is no open Polar sea.

II.

Seasons and orders
Send us forth:
I to the sunlit morning,
You to night and north.

Cloud shades the morning:
We go out alone —
Into the summer garden,
Into the pale moon.

Frost ends the summer:
As we move away –
I to the lamplit manor,
You to the northern sea.

Orders and seasons,
Part us at command –
I to the gold of autumn,
You to the silver land.

III.

The silence lasts, the distances remain,
The certainties of all the charts are lies,
No traveller knows the greatness of the cold.

The sky is broken looking glass in winter,
Capes of illusions, mirages of hills,
Offer vainglorious names for folds of air.

This is the realm of mirrors, what you bring
Into this region will return to you,
No traveller knows the greatness of the cold.

IV. THE DEAD CAPTAIN'S SONG

My words are spoken over frozen seas
Whispered in drift on ice and distances.
In winter dark I love my love alone

My only darling now is the frozen star
My only love is the knife edge of the wind.
All I desire lives at the winter's heart
In frost and silence on the glimmering plains

My words are spoken over frozen seas
Whispered in drift on ice and distances.
In winter dark I love my love alone

I will put on my shirt of new fallen snow
Aurora will light me, bridegroom to my bed,
Bring chosen by the north wind as her lover
To dwell there in devotion -- snow and bone.

My words are spoken over frozen seas
Whispered in drift on ice and distances.
In winter dark I love my love alone

V.

Cold England mourns in fog and fallen leaves
November twilight drowns bare avenues;
And all my life is evening since you are gone –
Rain in the dark, my long desolation.

O weeping England is a house of ghosts:
Voices at nightfall, whispers amongst dry leaves,
Shadows of young men lost amongst rocks and snows.

I am worse than a widow, I who can never marry –
Because you are not quite dead, I can never live:
So I must mourn through the stone rooms alone,
Embrace the frozen air that is all that can join us now.

VI.

Lord of the treasuries of Hail, absolve them now,
Queen of Miraculous Snowfall, lead them home.

Bright lichens quicken on their bones
The seashells strew their graves.
Those who sought to give names to silences,
Have offered to the silence their own names.

Snow flake and hoarfrost, *lie soft on them*
Snow-plume and frost flower, *grow for them*
Snow rose, ice briar, *bloom around them*

Ice-smoke, ice-mist, *fold them round*
Crystals of snowflakes, *grow for them*
Ice in the twilight, *staunch their wounds*

Snow flickering, darkness falling, *give them quiet*
Snow hovering, rime dissolving, *give them peace*
Snow distilled, frost manifest, *give them rest*

Have mercy, Lord of the glaciers and frozen seas;
Enfold them in your cloak, Queen of the Snows.

Lord of the treasuries of Hail, absolve them now;
Queen of Miraculous Snowfall, lead them home.

Traveller
Last August wind, dark pivot of the year
Our life can turn to winter in an hour.
Our strength can go, our friends be blown away,
Icefall or avalanche, unlucky storm,
For all our bravery, we end alone,
Alone like the poor bastard buried here.

Ghost
Cry blades, bleed lead, weep stone.
My veins are ice and stars
Eyes open below frozen ground.
Cry blades, bleed lead, weep stone

I died the death of lead
I live the death of stone.
Worst in these August days
Of short-lived sun:
The earth unfrozen,
Memory of light.

I'm stone now in a commonwealth of stones
With ice for blood, the granite at my heart;
Sea freezes, the sun passes to the south,
The last bird's cry has gone to silence now:
Meltwater of the month-long summer, flow.

Held here disconsolate, lost, cast away
North of the treeline, north of memory
I was alive and strong in shadows of the trees
was once as you are now, now overborne:
Water which rose in sunlight gone to stone.

Traveller
May the September snow descend and fold
About your wooden headstone on the shore
Falling in silence through the fading day

Aurora flare and move above your grave
In brilliance of gold and jade and rose
Over the desolation of the stones.

I grieve for you, for all of those the north
Holds in its cloudy prison of the snows.

Ships like great gulls left Kirkwall for the ice
By the far sea-roads they could not retrace

Those few came far to lay their bodies here
To hold a place in the green world no more

Ice thickens, daylight fails in winter cold
Dark save the starry guardians at the pole.

THE EARLY CHRISTIAN MONUMENTS OF WALES

Their world comes down to us as broken stones,
As wind worn monoliths in distant places.
The raindrop smooths the contours of the words,
The waterfall sounds nearer as evening draws on.

*

Sea mist on Anglesey, glistening roads to the shores.
The stone of King Cadfan, wisest, most famous of kings
Catamanus rex sapientissimus opinatissimus omnium regum
Rough letters, their lines faltering like an army retreating,
Like the fall of a wave from the stones of this westering strand.

*

The courteous guardian came with the church keys at evening:
The children call me Aunty Eglwys. The Lady Ecclesia
Is present in this silence, is formed in the whisper of this rain,
She who wept with her sister Synagogue at the foot of the Cross.

*

Think of the pillar stone on the clear hillside,
Spare upland trees, out in the light and the wind.
Concenn great grandson of Eliseg raised this stone
To that same Eliseg who took the realm of Powis from the English
Fragments of words, most of the lines gone now.
Vortigern, Maximus, titles of Monarchs and Emperors,
Maximus who took the flower of Britain away to the wars.
The blessing of God ... on the land of Powis until the Last Day.
Words growing thin in time's vastness, names themselves breaking,

Dissolving in rime and days through a thousand years,
Already faded when copied three hundred years past,
Still the river noise from the valley rises and dies as the wind goes.

*

Consider these monuments, these forgotten things,
Rain on the roofs of far, hill-folded churches,
Beyond the oak woods, down the stream-deep lanes,
The stone above unknowable on the bright hill.

*

Consider the devastating farness of the past.
Moving away from us like water in the dark
Swift mountain rivers flowing in the night under storm.
How can we comprehend our lostness and their clarity?
How can we know our darkness and their brightness?

LASTNESS, OR RORY'S APPLE

Hæc ostendit mihi Dominus Deus: et ecce uncinus pomorum.

A flooded, desperate January day. The great avenue at Cirencester hidden in bitter mist; the exquisite rooms chill and disordered. Strain and low light, worry and overwork, projects coming to nothing. After lunch, Rory brought us a basket of stored yellow apples, from an unnamed tree in his parents' orchard. From their house on the western shore, far into Wales, sold in November after the death of his mother, and the apples brought away on the last day there. They were right at the end of their time, pitted with rot, but, in the two good mouthfuls on each one, was all the past sweetness, all the clove pinks of lost summers.

VENICE GLASSES III

Considered Silence
Consider this in quiet as the last of the daylight departs from you,
Marking the faltering air which fades now from ash-grey to blue;
Fragile as Venice glasses, this transient cobweb of branches,
On the silvered outskirts of Europe, at cobalt frontiers of evening,
This world in the window so frail that one touched switch could destroy it –
Holding one moment of snow, before our day passes to dark.

SECRET THEATRES OF SCOTLAND

Ghost plays, enactments in remote places which position the spectator as ghost-seer. These treat of unfinished business, of the past reaching into the present, attempts at understanding when forgiveness is not possible.

So you might stand at cold dawn by the window of a castle in the Black Isle, where there is a rough drawing of a great stag scratched into the plaster behind the shutter, with the words *Lang befor daylicht, he began his flicht.* These scratched lines trap the air of the 1740s in that window embrasure, so that looking out into trees in dawn haar, shadows of men and horses would flicker at the edges of vision, departures with no promise of return, and when the spectator made their way alone down the tower stair and out into the frozen morning a voice would be singing in the empty kitchen about the men who never returned, about the Frasers, Hays, and Gordons lost or fled abroad in King James's wars.

Daylight haunting in Sutherland, or in the passes of the Cairngorm: an uncouth ragged companion, persistent, archaic in speech, desperate to tell of griefs, a relation of loyalties and disasters. A woman amidst a ruckle of stones at the turn of the track, speaking of houses burned, of killings in late, clandestine wars. A young man, incoherent with fatigue: the day when the horse-troops or the police-troops came. Resistance and defeat, ruined flight across the uplands. Once such words have been uttered, they cloud and complicate the beauty of the day. Tokens of remembered sorrow as summer begins to go over; words hanging like flakes of snow in far-blue August air.

*

In a mountain bothy, the walking ghosts of the climbers. On the high uplands, danger and the otherworld are as close as the shadows on the snow. The air in the bothy thickening with cold as the light on the snow fades beyond the little windows. No human cloud of warm breath in the light of the paraffin lamp, although the air is freezing, and there is a crowd around the rough table drinking drams and toasting the dead. Fragments of memory in their speech would piece together a story of footprints found after fresh snowfall, tracks which lead to the rotten ice under the snow crust, to the edge of the crevice.

*

Words diamond-scratched on a window pane three centuries ago can hold an angry ghost in an old room.

Suppose that you arrived at the lightless house on the edge of Edinburgh at nightfall, suppose you were met at the door by an anxious housekeeper or caretaker, with a flashlight. Suppose you were conducted up a dark staircase and through an enfilade of rooms in which dim shapes of shrouded furniture – dust sheets in a house closed up and abandoned – could just be made out by the light of the torch, by the lightspill from factories and streetlights seeping through the windows. The faintest notes of a harpsichord and hesitant voice sound in the farthest distance of the silent house, unheard by its custodian, who throws open the door of the room, saying that they must get home and that they will lock the house after you've gone. But they seem not to see that the room is lit and warm: a fire in the hearth, candles on the chimneypiece, two wing chairs set by the fire. You settle by the fire, perhaps taking a candle in its silver stick from the mantelpiece to examine the words on the window panes. The moment you come near to the window, murmurs begin in the corners of the room, from which a single voice emerges, a beautiful voice roughened by sorrow and loneliness and time, and the room fills with the thoughts of the woman who scratched the words into the glass. For an hour you hear it, and sometimes the voice dies, as the fire begins to sink on the hearth, but then it breaks into single words and silences as the candles burn down and the fire falls to ashes. A door slams far away in the empty house and then you are alone in the dark, the last candle a stub, and the lightwash of our own time becomes visible once more beyond the windows.

*

In a quiet town, in Cove or Helensburgh, there is an empty house with a view out to the long sunsets. Westwards over gardens and rooftops, down to water with hills rising from a distant shore. To enter the empty villa is to enter a theatre of whispers and memories. There are no curtains, nor furniture, only the slightest traces of the inhabitants of these rooms: a rose or a seashell on the ledge of a bedroom fireplace. Empty, afternoon rooms, voices murmuring in your ears about past time, about how a woman, felt, or once felt, about the events of a life; how events in the decades of that life had imprinted themselves on the way that the slate roofs shone in the rain one Sunday afternoon of low cloud and misunderstandings. How the morning had lain on the hills, when she was holding a child up to the window to see it for the first time. How the scent of bought chrysanthemums had filled the whole house with autumn and peace, the quiet last sunlight lying level on the waters to the west. So an accumulation of days grows in the end to a whole.

*

You arrive by the rough track high in bare Glenlivet. You are walking by the light of a head-torch across the narrow bridge over the burn, passing the hump of ruins where Cumberland's soldiers burned the old house: stone walls and a pair of rowan trees. Look around to see how bare the bowl of hills is, how sparse the trees are. You see how you have come to the end of all the roads, even the sheeptracks, and to go further, the only option would be, in every sense, to take to the heather. In short summer the hills blur in infinite blues. In autumn and winter, they are that scoured to a dun which is a negation of colour. Then the snows come.

You arrive at the darkened house, which comes alive in stirring and the light and scent of beeswax and bog-myrtle candles as you touch the handle of the door. A young man in the black clothes of three hundred years ago, holding his staff of office which is a narwhal's tusk mounted in silver, bows before you. A great carved chair is set for you by the turf fire in a long, low room, a glass of muscatel is poured for you, cakes of almond and orange-water are set at your elbow. A sacred drama is acted for you alone, by masked and golden-robed players speaking only in Latin. They enact renunciations of the world and, in the end, a martyrdom. Sometimes there is grave music sung in counterpoint, until at the last they break their slow decorum to cry aloud with joy and a curtain is thrown back and there is an apotheosis of the hero triumphant amidst clouds, crowned with stars, his palms and golden laurels lit by candleflames focused by mirrors and glass globes of water. Then the players put off their masks and come one by one in silence to kiss your hand as you sit in the great chair by the fire. And the steward comes again with his unicorn-cane to usher you into the dark.

The hills and the north about you, and time uncertain.

*

High summer midnight, shadowy with great trees
The oak leaves overhead sewn thick with stars,
Rügen offshore, and the wind soft through the groves.

'I know he would have come here as a child
To play among the ruins, so this place
Was at his heart.'
                              'And that great arch?'
'It is the gate of the greenwood, Peter, if you should choose,
Beyond it lie all the April mornings of the 1820s;
It is the door to gentle democracies under the soft brown moon
To the sun through the pinewood at the end of a life lived well.
Or else it is the way to the past and the forest in winter,
To the lonely, unforgotten thorns on the heath outside Dresden,
The desolate whaleback monoliths on the Baltic shore,
And ice seas north of everything where oppressions thrive.'

'Sophie, this arch, this portal of the snows and the stars:
It is so many things, we hardly dare pass through it.'

EVENINGS UNDER THE LINDEN TREE

For Mark Gibson

Here in the linden sweetness so deep in the summer of Germany
Soft Baltic air flows from the north and the sea;
I stay for you, distant and past, beloved familiar phantoms.

I wait in this darkening garden as lamps are brought forth in the castle,
To the room which forms in mirrors and girandoles as the music begins;
The handsome wanderer, the Englishman slouched in the corner,
Gazes in lamplight on daughters in summer night muslin.
Music through open windows, breath of *L'Heure Bleu* under vast boughs,
The long-dead Countess comes to me here in the shades of the garden,
O Linden my refuge, Acacia Tree my interpreter,
Murmur of summer, assure me that nothing is done with and gone.

Midnight and stillness, the warm dark heavy with sweetness,
Then the half-breath at last, the ghost-kiss, affinity of air:
As if wedded phantoms return from two hundred years past,
Those who gazed together into tall glasses in sparse rooms
Who sang in the evenings by lamplight at the square piano.
Suppose you descended like dew to the shadowy garden,
You who were faithful here, you who are now in Elysium:
Hesitate, should you revisit, no, whisper it, no, do not break it.

Under the lime leaves, under the westering stars, through this sweet breath
        of the lindens,
Pass, most fortunate ghosts, through this late evening of summer.

MR DOWLAND'S MIDNIGHT

Vivens tacebam: mortua canto

Look out upon these candles of the air
Whose small lights fall with this last day which brings
Us and our summers closer to their west
Through these dimmed valleys and the shooting stars.
So we have moved all day within this grove
Testing the lindens' virtues, marking down
Which trunks make lute-wood, noting the sounding trees.

Small lights attend our wanderings in this place
Perseids and fireflies, glimmers like torches move
Below in the wood where the dead lovers go.
I may lament, but cannot sing them home
No more than one dim taper light a shire.

So late. I hardly touch the fret to shape
Your face's praises from the moving air,
One finger's pressure measuring the string;
All strength is holding back: which truth being known,
The heart unharboured now, the poplar wood
Sings under sound, half-silent beats of air,
And the lute's soul goes forth, bearing discourse
(*Vivamus mea Lesbia)* into night.

SEPTEMBER CASTLES

First hints of our condition manifest:
Spite in the wind, mist-gauze across the moon,
Light chill, the spider's filaments, blanched grass,
And two days as warm as the south change nothing at all,
A morning comes when you know this cannot end well.
Soon it will be no time for gathering in gardens
All too soon, my dears, it will be the weather
For Brahms quintets, for leaves drifting *triste* past the windows
Of those in their rooms alone for the duration,
For whom this is no time to build. Those now alone
Are going to remain so through this estranging season
Of reading, of writing emails as detailed as letters,
Of watching dry leaves grow sodden on empty pavements.
Rilke said this in lines that I last read in Edinburgh
With my most beautiful aunt in her later age
When, many things gone, she remembered those verses in German.

DIALOGUE IN AUTUMN

Arisen from the groundwater of tears
We see this land as in our own reflections.
"On mist blue levels, in the shadowed farms,
The people sleep, their folded flocks about them."

We walk at night and ground mist folds around us
Our hair turns silver silently as moonlight.
"The water shivers, trains pass far away,
This grass smells chill with sap of trodden nettles."

Time passes, all things pass with us to silence,
Save those last things we see with eyes of childhood.
"The crimson roses drop like mottled coxcombs,
Our gardens cannot hold their scents much longer."

After Maurice Gilliams

LONDON BLUES

Smoke at the window, ghosts on the radio,
Cold in the dusk and the sound of the city below,
As the rose of the evening goes over gentle and slow.

Desolate western sky where the red sun shone,
Flicker of streetlights, lamps in long windows come on,
I loved one love alone and my love is gone.

Dust and scarlet ache in the wasting day,
My love stole into the crowd and vanished away,
And I ask of the fallen sun that one shadow should stay.

Crowds on the pavements break and falter and flow,
My love is gone among them, though I know
All the byways and narrow lanes where we used to go.

Cobalt blue city below the frost,
Twilight passing, hope and luck both past –
Black dark, evening star, and my darling lost.

PRAYER TO THE VIRGIN ON A WINTER NIGHT

Bomber's moon.
I have known
In stucco London lostness and loss alone.

Blackout.
Two hours' joy,
Sleeps gentle on my breast the spent brute boy.

Iron night.
Midnight
Past now, love works this transient delight.

Antipathies
Jealousies
Love turns such curious beauty out of these.

Cold planets move
In orbit above
This broken peace, my lover not my love.

Crowned with searchlights,
Crowned with stars,
Look down in pity on our sins and wars.

CON SORDINO

That night she whispered 'you're a prince in bed'
The window panes were blinded with frost-flowers;
Dead tired, we lay between the freezing sheets
Snow fell through darkness on the roofs and towers.

And by this snow the world is made again,
I am a child once more, born of this night,
Be gentle with my innocence, whose quiet
Voice is a picture from a Book of Hours.

See the blanched castle rise beyond the pines,
See, in blue distance, how a slanting ray
Of sunlight on the faithful landscape breaks.

A lady and a knight pass on their way
He whistles to the hounds, she sees the hawk,
Soar from her glove through fathoms of bright day.

After Martinus Nijhoff

AGAINST THE VANITY OF THE POETS

This is the desolate month, month of reproaches and mourning,
Death-bag November, gaslighting out of the darkness,
Whispering there is no voice which can outlive the silence;
Whispering there is no name, though lovely, beloved in season,
Of which the echo's not faint now and faded to nothing.
Dark our inheritance: all our bad grandfathers left us
Riven from those who could not defend their possession;
From all those they cast out bereft, that we might relish
Rainy quintets at evening, things which can never console us,
In this the desolate month, month of reproaches and mourning.

PRYDE'S GHOST

Invocation:
Out of the blue mist in this glass of gin,
From rough throat coalsmoke of the Lowland towns,
By the lost soldiers and the trodden snow:
Jimmy Pryde, I summon you.

Dismissal:
By gunsmoke and frost-thorns brought together,
At drop of day when the harrow looses,
Through the worn theatres of the London sky:
Jimmy Pryde, I send you home.

THE SUPPER

Silence at table, as if bread and wine,
Dropped from our strengthless hands. The guttering
Candle flames stammered, failed. Blown in,
The casement slammed in violent wind that night.

And far below the house old realms, like waters,
Stirred in the dark. We all felt the gale,
Seize on us then, it filled the driven sails
Blowing us to our deaths, driving time's flight.

You cannot hide yourself in company
Alone, you see your own bleak loneliness
Reflected deeper in another's eyes.

So when the long winds howl above the town
Forget, forget all that your weak hearts mourn:
Laugh, and clash crystal glasses till they shatter.

After Martinus Nijhoff

SPEECHES IN A PARK IN THE NORTH, IN WINTER

For Louisa and Tristram

HE
My mirrors troubled and the winter near
I have crossed plains of adamant and dust
In failing day, in this hunter's season,
Under a sanguine, westering sun.
I dream myself benighted in a place
Of restless waters and unchaste despair.

SHE
And light which falls is light as sure to soar
(Aurora wanton over tumbled snow).
The windows glimmer with our diamond names,
We kindle in pavilions of bright air
The sweet new fire born from the starry trees
In towers and plumes of scarlet and of snow.

REX WHISTLER'S BLUES, AUGUST 1938

How soon these August evenings go
How slowly now the mornings come
As summer closes down. My show here's done
And my show's a good show, I know that now.
I've done the best thing here I'll ever do.

I've made a world, all summer in a day,
And under the arcade at the shadow end,
I've painted myself as the dark gardener's boy
The fag-end of summer, that's where I belong.

I who have known by heart the poetry
Of lovely, fugitive, expensive things:
The swish cars whispering down October roads,
Venetian mirrors, dances, hothouse flowers
Lights of great houses fading like music at dawn.

What will I leave behind? No house, no heir.
A ghost of a pale profile at a window
A thrown-back forelock, a flick of inky hair
Shading dark eyes. But all these things
Are threads like cigarette smoke in cold air –
Because dawn broke with my words to my love unspoken
Long winter's coming, gunsmoke in frozen air.

I leave behind this painted world, I leave
My shadow on the wall for when we're gone
Sweeping the fallen petals of the rose,
And the good days are fading like smoke and soon they'll be over —
The swallows muster at the summer's close;
My good days are smoke on the wind and soon they'll be done.

*

THE MUSEUM OF LOSS

The Museum of Loss has no permanent home: its collections are always on tour, sometimes on show in more than one location at once. Things restless of their nature, disquieted and melancholy, objects borne down by a burden of memory too grave to sustain. It was to contain these that the Museum came into being.

The Museum has no website, publishes no maps, offers no directions to visitors. When it has halted and set forth its exhibits, the Museum never advertises its presence, save in ways noticed only by those predisposed to see them. There are, however, conditions in which the Museum is more likely to be found.

Winter dusk, prickle of frost, coal in the air, smoke in the throat.

Lesser streets of provincial towns, railway arches, smudged brick, flaking stone.

River-harbour, fog, ships' sirens, splinters of glass and ice between cobbles.

*

Latest summer, sullen and overblown, thunderstorms coming. A fair on the outskirts of a country town.

Cut grass on the drainage ditches, level horizons, murmur of insects, heaviness of trees.

Vapour of petrol, mechanical music, arc lights and sodium flares.

*

Outermost London, failing parade of shops, overshadowed autumn day.
Faltering end of afternoon, rain setting in, tyres on wet asphalt.
One shop with a light behind a whited-out window.

*

Late spring, hill road, long views of cold slopes and shores, far bitter wind.
Cardboard arrows, tracks which are only a scatter of cobbles in matted grass, rusted gates and fallen stone posts.
A croft or field barn, alone on that scarred hillside.

The visibility of the Museum depends on the state of the visitor. Unease and longing are the moods to which it will disclose itself. Or a degree of fever, illness coming on. An aimless walk, undertaken as a late distraction, may end at the door of the Museum. Those more robust, more anchored in the present, will stride past and never see its sign, never guess that it has almost brushed against them.

The curatorial staff are highly qualified for their posts: they seem inconsolable. Hence the weary perfection of their manners, the sincerity of their expressions of regret.

The collections policy of the Museum is governed by the dictum WHAT IS TO BE FEARED ABOUT OBJECTS IS LESS THEIR SILENCE THAN THEIR ELOQUENCE. The disposition of the Museum's cases is governed by hierarchies of displacement. And always the sense that there is a perfect place for the display of any one object, and that that place is elsewhere.

There is no museum shop. Visitors will appreciate that absence.

Opening hours: *belated, benighted.*

Price of admission: in one sense, *free.* In another, *at a price.*

*

OF DEATH, FAME AND IMMORTALITY

And so she died, her crystal rosary wreathed about hands white as though
        they were marble already,
Pale, rain-glimmering briars wound about columns of snow.
Her husband looked forth into violet and silver of twilight,
We are breath on cold glass, we are wind-blown smoke, we are nothing.

It was far into Cumberland, beyond the mountains, late in the autumn,
The swans had long passed over through cloud-wrack of shadow and sable,
        harried
on gales out of Ireland.

So the question arose how to mourn one who had been so much loved,
How her household might give voice to their loss and devotion;
For strictures from distant London prohibited customary rituals, the words
        of old comfort,
And all that remained was for each to make verse of their grief.

They ordered a canopy of carpenter's work to be raised where she lay in the
        stone hall,
Which ardent chapel was also their castle of sorrow.
A winter's worth of wax tapers blazed there on high for one evening,
The papers of verses being fastened below to the columns,
When the carriages came after nightfall in crackle of frost over gravel.

Some knelt and their hands dropped pearls and gold for a moment,
Others stood, heads bowed, then read the marvellous verses –
Parterres of her virtues, orchards of her charity –
A rose from the hand of Aurora, cast down, overborne amongst snows.
When the last had departed, they laid her in the bare chancel in silence.

It was a shadowed time, an unpropitious time, remote, in a place of no
        consequence,
A manor lost beyond drowned furrows and sodden impassable roads.

Her daughter, forty winters after, in the convent parlour at Antwerp,
Burnt the papers of verses to ashes — cold light in the brick streets outside,
        the cranes
crying over the rooftops.
She was old and at peace and had done with the things of this world.

Roses fall, summers go over. Nothing can ever recover them.
Their strew of mourning verses is as lost as last rain-spattered August,
Whose ardours and beauties would have been wonders of Europe.

GLASGOW, 10 MARCH 1615

Through shadows, from the drift of history,
Out of torn Europe in an evil time,
Alone and not alone, you carried home
Your hidden name, your secret heraldry.

Forsaken Captain, glorious in your loss,
Broken in triumph, dead in victory;
Your love could force the great ones of your day
To go in fear of your humility.

What is it like -- this love, this clarity?
It is yet purer than the airs that pass
Over your frozen hills beyond the Spey;

More brilliant than white sunlight on white ice;
It moves as freely through our hearts as fine
Wind from the snowline, like a blade, like Grace.

ST EDMUND CAMPION MEDITATES ON THE PASSION

The honest soldiers stammer in their dreams
This air which stirs at dawn is all they feel
Smoke and the shadows forming all they see.

The fire is lit and straw laid in the garden
All for my wedding, and no rose for You
But weaves its thorns to hurt your tangled hair.

Falcon and knife are keenest in the daybreak
With level steps You climb the morning sky:
Our sanguine banner braves all common day.

THE TRUE VINE

Virescit vulnere virtus

Learning from childhood the culture of vines, I follow each part of this
          metaphor:
No vine can flower on old timber, new shoots only grow after pruning,
But then you must cut them, allow the sky into the branches,
Thin out the clusters that follow, or rot takes them late in the season.
My grandfather's villa was heavy with the scents of olive and vine –
Sharp oil and olive-wood smoke;
And sour heavy air from the cellars, grape must and ullage of wine.
Beyond the cypress gardens, were the bleached grounds of parched earth and
          olive trees,
Salt on the evening wind, vines on the landward slopes, below the dust-
          shimmering hills.
There it was always late in the day, heat in the air pressing down,
Sorrow and thunder, the heat haze hiding the mountains,
Last migraine days of late summer, with the new wine unquiet in its barrels,
Working under the slumbering villa.

Many years later, and far to the north, I mended a ruinous vine-house:
The leaves and the black Hamburg grapes sharp against white nights of
          summer.
There my wine-merchant cousin taught me to manage the vine-shoots,
How the stem lives for ever, comes back from the darkness each year,
While the shoots are ephemeral,
And must be pruned hard after Easter, if they are to flower in the light,
And pruned at midsummer again, with the light on the northern horizon,
If the grapes are to fill with the darkening rains in September.
But here you must never make wine,
You lie far too far to the north,
Where the soil tastes of apples and coal,
And the vine and its fruit are in exile.

I have studied the vine-emblem long: *virescit vulnere virtus*
The sorry baroque of a church and a country divided:
The Queen of England is childless, a branch to be pruned for the burning,
The Queen of Heaven's sweet likeness was gashed by the pikemen at Cadiz;
All love then broken, the vine turned token of treason.
Only the poet-saint in hiding
Sang how we are lopped back on earth that we may flourish forever,
How those whose end is worldly failure grow like vines and rose-trees in
        heaven:
The incense smoke sweet in still air, the bud of the eglantine blown.

Look about now:
May goes out softly, hawthorn flowers dry to brown dust,
Elderflowers constellate, roses blow red on the wall.
The willow-cloud has passed over, the soft leaves trail in the waters,
Along the green reaches of river, briar rose and bramble-flower open,
Spread their enamel-work petals over their cut-work of branches.

All things move to their vintage, in the cathedral still after Trinity,
Motes in the sun at the open west doors, bird-shadows flowing in azure.
In the parched gardens of August, grapes ripen, roses flower on,
Days move sweetly under the heavens.
Through this late prodigious summer, of continuance and holding in love;
In life as in metaphor, in all my small works I move forward,
Under my late-pruned vine-arbour in the town garden;
And I will do so (by the mercy of God)
Through the years of quiet harvests, through all my remaining Septembers.

SONNET FOR TRINITY SUNDAY

Dog rose and elder blossom for Trinity Sunday,
Hornbeam leaf, emblem of greenness renewed at this season;
High summer brilliance of green over wasteland and garden,
Poised in its balance still, but thread-thin frail:
Quick this could parch, waste, diminish, wither away.
But slow clouds sail high now, cloud bloom spreads on the elder.
Quickened by fall of grace, by soft rain on the river
Which whispers in leaf-dim twilight under the trees.

Where does all greenness begin? The Trinity
Is spring, source, strength, and return. And how may we
Honour our debt, when debt is so great to pay?
Only by co-creation which tends and attends,
For we are God's hands and eyes through each green day
Of dog rose and elder, plough-furrowed leaf of the hornbeam.

THE THIRD LAND

Singing, unburdened by memory,
I came out of the first land;
Singing, unburdened by memory

I went into the second land.
Oh God, I did not know my way
When I came into this land.

Oh God, I do not know my way,
But let me go forth on my way,
And let me, unburdened by memory,

And singing, enter the third land.

After Martinus Nijhoff

THE SECRET JOURNEY, ADDRESSED TO OUR LADY

Secretum iter fallentibus semita vitae

You who will receive these words at evening, at the hour when the starlight
          kindles in your apartments,
If there is evening as such where you dwell, where the stars are one light with
          the rose-gold of dawn,
Your feathered retinue glimmering below in the courtyards, singing in
          whispers like the plume-fall of your fountains,
Whose counterpoint is one with the perpetual canon of the stars, which is as
          much the zone of music as of flowing light or water,
Where light itself is of magnitude beyond experience.
How might I lay before you disquiets of this transient estate, cumulative
          failures of courage: postponements, omissions, half-hearted,
          belated arrivals?
A retrograde journey through backwoods; dim uplands, by single-track hill-
          roads;
Obscurity always the refuge, time and ability squandered, true things
          neglected for trifles:
wilderness of days wracked, cabinet of shadows;
At the end of all contemplations in exile, true ache of perception of exile, of
          want of the golden city,
So I must hope in your love for those who are wanting in love; to commend
          me to my Lord your Son, whose countenance I long for in the
          close.

CANTICLES FOR GOOD FRIDAY

Porfirizado de tu sangre,
Coronado de rosas morenas

I

Your silence is the stillness before day
Your blood drops as the rain on parching earth;
My Lord is wounded as my Lord is still
Your wounds are eloquent beyond all words.

Glory of porphyry,
Purple of blood;
Dolorous roses
Of the dark briar.
My sins are your wounds –
My sorrow, your glory.

II

O wounded beauty in eclipse,
O folds of snow to hold the Holy Face,
From dirt of the road, from soil of our sins –
Our consolation and our sorrow now.

III

The tree takes living flame, the dry staff flowers,
And flower and fire are the death of our death.
Drop balsam, weep in incense, flare in blood:
There blows upon your stock the wounded rose.

Tree most exalted,
Soften your branches;
Hardwood grow tender,

Gently embrace him;
Gently enfold him,
Cradle Him dying –
O softly fold your dying Creator round,

IV.

For love I tended you in paradise,
My people, raised you as the chosen vine
In my heart's vineyard guarded you from harm
With adamant and steel you pierced my heart.

Parched in the arid chasm of the sands
In pity for your thirst I made flint weep,
Flow crystal and pour diamond from the stone.
With adamant and steel you pierced my heart.

O Heart dissolve in blood, eyes melt in tears:
Wine of my vineyards will flow forth for you,
My stars will draw the rain to your starved land

Fountain of pity, desolate joy,
Daystar rising, rose of morning;
Love of my wounded heart
Our tears and blood are one.

V.

Darkness about us in the failing day
Stark desolation, night at the third hour,
And our most lasting things are works of sand.
Only the river from your wounded side
Can clean the earth and seas, can scour the stars:
Ark on black water, last and only hope,
Sole harbour from the shipwreck of this world.

Fountain of pity, desolate joy,
Daystar rising, rose of morning;
Love of my wounded heart
Our tears and blood are one.

PER GRAZIA RICEVUTA TO OUR LADY OF ABERDEEN

You who are flame and lantern, tears and air,
Infinite forbearance on the homeward road;
You who are sea foam and August snow,
Mother and daughter of the morning star;

For the young woman benighted in desperate uplands of winter,
For the young man shot from behind by the bullet of clotted blood,
For those who went untimely, yet by your grace returned, receive these verses.

It was as though she was lost amidst frost and thorns,
On the stone shoulder of the moor, night and strong cold coming on,
Walking in circles, seeing the lit house in the valley,
Who went unwilling, yet by your grace returned.

It was as though he had descended into the maze of the twilight,
Moth-wing dusk of the labyrinth, Aeneas gone into the dark,
A thread his only path, the spark of your taper his guide,
Who went unwilling, yet by your grace returned.

She stands homecoming at the gate and the lights of the house are bright in
          soft dusk for her;
He comes in from the dark garden (hair drenched with rain from the roses)
          and all will be well and as it was.

For you are flame and lantern, tears and air,
Infinite forbearance on the homeward road;
For you are sea foam and August snow,
And Mother of the morning star.

THE MOURNING VIRTUOSO

I

Your lovers knew you least, your friends hardly at all:
Your fictions grew denser the closer in we came,
Like a labyrinth overgrown at the centre, a maze in a palace garden, well to
the east of the
Elbe, a place that has changed its name often;
As tangled, for example, as the far-off, shagged gardens of the Prince Bishop
of Olomouc.

You were very brilliant and very ill, that was the nugget of truth, where
everything else was a fiction:
Falsehoods of your pasts, of your family, your languages, your studies,
Meshes of fabrication like a dazzle of fireworks moving very fast across the
night sky of Europe;
Or feigned nostalgias for things that never were, devastating longings for
unvisited places,
Like dreamy sleeping cars, decades ago, clicking past moonstruck
uncomprehending villages.

When I visited you in your last, your fortieth, year
You seemed the lame tutelar of empty late-summer London,
(Your silver-topped stick stirring blown sand in old alleyways)
The limping genius of the deserted City, of the thick air of sad August
evenings,
Guardian of the slashed-sale shirtmakers, of deserted city churches;
Of the unfrequented, middle-price restaurants in dust-shabby streets,
With their bored and handsome waiters, very worked-out, very bored.
Then our halting walk home, as Hesperus flaunted in cobalt over St Paul's,
And sparse constellations of lamps showed in high flats in the Barbican,
Where you brooded over London from your beautiful rooms, every object
with its lie, with its falsified history:

A provenance in Vienna apartments, or a moribund house in the midlands of
    Ireland.
How seldom we think to question what a close friend tells us for true:
Your lovers knew you least, your friends hardly at all.

And so I must shape myself one last time for you, as the Mourning Virtuoso,
Being in a sense chosen for office, executor of one of your wills,
Invested by your gift of a seal-ring, clasped hands cut in carnelian,
Hellenistic, from the Cavafy period, from the time of the failure of kingdoms.
So I must write your elegies which must be as plural as you were plural,
And complicated, oh yes, complicated, fluid, twisty, vertiginous;
There are times, my desolate children, when baroque's your only man.

II

Most often, and to most, you offered histories of exile,
The vast, dark, landlocked Empire at your back—
The stations washed Emperor's yellow from the Great Mountains down to
    Trieste;
In late nineteenth century summer turning to glimmering autumn,
Rain from the east, like arrows on lead roofs of the far-scattered castles –
The remotest, the furthest, the deepest into the forests,
Mirroring drops of water on leaves by the sides of long single-track railways,
    all of which led to Vienna.
And your grandparents in Vienna, you said, civilised people who went to the
    theatre, to the *Hofoper*
(Technocrats, industrialists, with interests in plywood and mineral springs)
The fictions always prudently general, never shooting too high,
They attended first nights, but did not claim to know the composers,
And always had business in London, so that they could leave,
Quietly with assets intact, at the first signs of trouble in Europe.
You took one risk once, with a lover studying psychiatry,
This teacup was given to my aunt by Anna Freud
And the question arose of why and on what occasions
Did people in such circles give each other single Meissen teacups?

Which you evaded by evoking childhood visits with your mother (tea with
		lemon, *Linzer Torte*)
To autumnal streets of Hampstead, citadel of displacements and nostalgias,
Of broken twigs scuttering across the broad avenues of the exiles;
And your imagined Grandfather saying *we speak every language of Europe in
		this house, except, of course, German.*
O skeleton leaves blown from the Empire: remembrances, secrets,
		Konditoreien, regrets—
This, to lament you duly, must lament also that history.

III

Dark baroques of the long vacations, rumours and disappearances,
Hints of discreet excavations, secret assignations with antiquity,
Divisions of spoils by the light of the headlamps. White linen suit pockets
Simply rattling with intaglios, golden *fibula* stuck in your hatband.
Invitations to tenebrous, distant colloquia, in unverifiable small cities:
Jugendstil boulevards, grainy coffee and *lokum*, white dust, attar of roses;
Shabby half-criminal *savants*, travelled from further east still
With objects to sell for hard currency, their provenance quite irrecoverable
From castles beyond the rivers, before the wars, so far in far regions.
Or so you said on return, tuning your tale to your hearers,
Bearing in triumph to Bond Street the spoils of conquered Dacia.
Which paid in part for the perfect clothes, the London dinners.
The clouds of *Habit Rouge* in the bleak university corridor.

There were (maybe true) relations of scholarly Levantine summers
Slow sifting dust and detritus, last umbrages of Empires,
Scratched vestige of writings, a sorcerer's gem stone, Thoth's ibis on a crystal.
Not too often, and operating in territories too remote for corroboration,
You introduced small improvements to the past, micro-fictions,
Bizarre dispatches on consummate postcards signed off in Coptic:
As the skull bashed in behind the serene Fayum portrait
Of that charming young man who bears on his forehead a star.

You conjured an August romance with a murderer's son, in a mill-house in
           Gloucestershire,
After which you left with us a box of his letters "for safety, for discretion"
And were furious to discover that we had not so much as glanced at them.
Then you claimed a summer in a mountain clinic for a rare disease inherited
           in the female line:
As though you were not always ill in truth, almost too ill to have gone to
           school at all,
Despite your Protean, comic-erotic *Bildungsroman* of your education.

But you had to be starkly ill before your friends saw your apartments,
Spacious modernist rooms; perfect arrangements of imperfect objects;
And now and then, never there twice, some stupendous antiquity.
How seldom we come to question what a close friend tells us for true:
This to lament you duly, must lament also these shadows.

IV

Rainy evening, Manchester, *une boîte amusante*, an urgent whisper:
I am somebody else here, I am a music producer,
My name's on this card, we're staying at the Lowry,
I am not the person here you think you knew elsewhere,
I am somebody else here, we're staying at the Lowry.
I'll buy you dinner there, but you must use the name on this card,
I am a music producer, not the person you thought you knew elsewhere.
This to lament you duly, must lament also those evenings.

V

It sometimes seems as though there were a city of fictitious personal histories
(A place so intensely imagined that it acquires a shadow existence),
The native place claimed by urbane men (such as you were) whose childhoods
           must never be mentioned:
A lost European capital in a high old time of experiment and lavishness in
           the arts,
An era of *fiacres* and swish cars moving slowly down boulevards of chestnuts
           and lilacs,

Of cream-filled chocolates scented with hothouse flowers:
Tuberose, stephanotis, frangipani, orange blossom and jasmine.
All mothers were widows there, vast hats, black silks and nosegays of violets,
Rose-cut diamonds and pearls glimmering through veils of black spotted
       voile,
Closed car to the opera, the philharmonic, the quartets in the palaces.
All in an era between obliterating conflicts: all fathers had been officers (so
      handsome in their portraits) and all had been killed,
So there were no adult masters at the Lyceum, nor at the Archbishop's
      Gymnasium,
Only the old, unseeing professors born in the years before the wars,
And young, tow-haired fencing instructors, legitimate objects of conquest.
To lament you duly, this too must lament that city which never existed.

VI

How seldom we come to question what a close friend tells us for true:
You kept all your fables in motion like glittering shards in the air
Above the long table set for your fortieth birthday,
And you sustained it – a glass-feather chandelier held in being by
      conjuration,
Fugue-fountain glimmering all evening, splintering fragments of self;
So that each guest thought their host the person they knew alone.
The counterpoint twisted on, virtuosity twined with abandon,
Voices piled upon voices, risks grown outrageous, reckless gratifications.
Unstoppable fugue of your lives in your life, how to sustain them strength
      failing,
Hands shaking, will failing, strands tangling, breaking. Then at daybreak
One morning you and all your selves were gone.

VII

Forth from such broken selfhood where could the soul go?
Into which purgatory of delinquent mirrors, into which aftermaths and
      dissolving places?

Which regions like fairgrounds under white rain in the wastes outside our
        lives?
Zones far as the farthest peripheries of cities, seen from the railway, seen at
        nightfall from the cold stopping train:
Goods yards and sidings, lostness and drifting, arc-lights and ebb tides,
Foreshore, landfill, hoardings and scaffolding, staked plots on unmade roads,
Craters and builders' rubble, moon rainbows of oil in groundwater, spoil
        heaps of sand.
With the empty, lit buses that will never stop, circling these margins all night,
Bright as carnival floats on darkling wet roads, carrying with them away
All of your beautiful, sad, contemptuous fictions:
All those who you were not, nor had been, and all those you never could be.

How can the soul make its way through this static, these funfairs and buzzing
        wires,
This white noise, this magnesium flare, this drenched apparitional garden,
Out of this shifting region (yet your fabrication) how can stillness come?
Who could from this place draw peace, know wholeness, or find glory?

How can you be drawn forth into singleness, into quiet, reparation, and light?
Perhaps though persistence in memory and devotion alone,
(Like making this *Grabschrift* which has, off and on, taken the best part of a
        decade.)
So I will remember you in continuance of hope,
Until you come to the place distilled by relentless love
Where the martyr and the pursuivant embrace
And the silver doves brood in the trees of paradise.

St Michael and All Angels, 2020.

ELEGY FOR CHARITY CHARITY

(1959–2021)

White swans on the green stream, why did you come
So close at evening to the house where she
Lay past all words but poetry?
Were you love's earliest messengers to call her home?

Star flowers of elder drifting on the grass
In wind-blown constellations: does the sweet
Heaven cast itself before her feet,
Carpeting earth with Perseids wherever she might pass?

Soft voices in the hours before the day
Murmur about the sleeping house: are these
Love's latest emissaries,
His private music sent to attend her on her way?

Starlight in shadowed waters mirroring far,
Starlight amidst green branches, lit by love
To shine below, to blaze above,
To shroud her in sweet laurel leaves and the high summer stars.

FATHER WILLCOCK'S EVENING HYMN

Unfold your kingdoms in the western sky,
Your transient citadels of ash and rose;
Disclose no more,
Your chain of mercies which has shaped our day.

Enfold us in the shadows of your hours,
Within your counterpoints of fading light;
Compose our night
All vast and far in consonance of stars.

That I with all below may raise my heart;
More fortunate than I can hope or know,
If so I may
In your great consort bear but the lowest part.

Jacobite Song and *Lord Derwentwater's Rose* were set to music by Paul Mealor in 2012. The Jacobite Earl of Derwentwater, executed after the rising of 1715, was informally venerated as a martyr by Roman Catholic families in the north of England. The phrase 'the best, most injured King' comes from Derwentwater's last letter before his execution.

Venice Glasses, the section titles are the names of complex, wonderful and allusive paintings by my friend Victoria Crowe.

Catterline is a versification of a conversation with my friend John Morrison, son of the late painter James Morrison, in which he remembered in detail being a child in the early 1960s, amongst the group of artists who lived in the cliff-top village of Catterline, south of Aberdeen. One of them, Angus Neil, suffered from PTSD after service in WWII. The verse was written as a gift for John's birthday.

Macnaughtan's Bookshop, Haddington Place, Edinburgh was originally published in *Off the Shelf: a Celebration of Bookshops in Verse*, ed. Carol Ann Duffy (London: Picador, 2016)

Shakespeare's Winter's Tale is a version of *Shakespeare's Winteravondsprookje* by the Dutch poet Martinus Nijhoff (1894-1953); there are versions of Nijhoff throughout this collection.

Arctic Elegy draws material from an oratorio of the same name set to music by Ed Jones and first performed in 2015 in St Andrew's Cathedral, Aberdeen.

74 degrees North: a dialogue at a grave, draws material from the libretto of a chamber opera *74 degrees North* with music by Paul Mealor and electro-acoustic soundscape by Pete Stollery, performed by Scottish Opera in 2010.

The Early Christian Monuments of Wales is a sequence of reflections on first millennium Christian inscriptions still in place in Wales. Sections of this were set for baritone and electro-acoustic pre-recorded soundscape, by Pete Stollery (as *Lost Princes*) in 2013, commissioned and performed by Jeremy Huw Williams.

Lastness, or Rory's Apple: the epigraph is from Amos, Chapter 8, 1. "Thus hath the Lord GOD shewed unto me: and behold a basket of summer fruit."

Dialogue at Kloster Eldena is a record of a visit, with Dr Sophie Dietrich, to the ruined abbey near Greifswald which recurs in Caspar David Friedrich's paintings throughout his life. It is a tribute to Sophie's beautiful and original doctoral dissertation on *Seasonal Variation in the Landscape Art of Baltic Germany and Scandinavia*

Evenings under the Lime Tree is a set of variations on the poem of the same title by Ludwig Kosegarten which was twice set to music by Schubert.

September Castles is a variation on Rilke's poem *Herbsttag*.

Pryde's Ghost remembers the Scottish painter of nightmares and ruins James Pryde (1866-1941).

Rex Whistler's Blues : the society painter Rex Whistler painted a remarkable illusionistic mural at Plas Newyyd in Anglesey in the late 1930s, while he was unhappily in love with his patron's daughter. He painted his self-portrait into the mural, dressed as a servant. He was killed in WWII.

*

Of Death, Fame and Immortality is based on fragmentary indications that a Catholic family in Cumberland in the late c16 marked the death of the Squire's wife with the kind of ceremonial, including papers with poems pinned to the hearse, with which a continental magnate would have been mourned. From 1560 to the 1830s it was in varying degrees illegal to be a practising Catholic in Britain.

Glasgow, 10 March, 1615 was the place and day of the martyrdom of St John Ogilvie, a Jesuit priest from the northeast of Scotland whose earlier life is still not fully known.

St Edmund Campion meditates on the Passion St Edmund Campion was martyred in London on 1 December 1581. The juxtaposition of his martyrdom and the Passion and Resurrection of Christ is found in St Robert Southwell's 1590s poem 'Christ's Bloody Sweat.'

The True Vine won *proxime accessit* in the Oxford University Prize for an English Poem on a Sacred Subject in 2019. References are to the ritual vandalization of a statue of the Virgin during Essex's raid on Cádiz in 1596, and to St Robert Southwell's poem 'Decease, Release.' My mother's Anglo-Spanish family were merchants at Cádiz.

Sonnet for Trinity Sunday was written for the *Laudato Sí* Institute at Campion Hall, Oxford in June 2021. It is based on a Trinity Sunday homily by Fr Matthew Dunch SJ.

Canticles for Good Friday were partly set to music by Paul Mealor in his Oratorio *Crucifixus*, first performed in 2012, and published by Novello.

Father Willcock's Evening Hymn was written in friendship for the Australian composer Fr Christopher Willcock SJ, when he was Visiting Fellow at Campion Hall, University of Oxford.

I am much in the debt of my friends Fiona Stafford, Andrew Biswell, and Will Ghosh for reading this collection in draft, and of my friend Rick Verhagen for much kind help with the versions from the Dutch.